VIOLINJUDY'S

THE ACCIDENTAL AXOLOTL

INTRODUCING SHARPS, FLATS & NATURALS

SUPPLEMENTARY SONGS
FOR BEGINNING-INTERMEDIATE PIANO LEARNERS

VERY FUN PIANO COLLECTION

The Accidental Axolotl by Judy Naillon

Copyright © 2023 ViolinJudy

www.violinjudy.com

ISBN: 978-1-960674-29-6

Violin Judy's

VERY FUN PIANO LIBRARY

Accidental Axolotl is composed for LEVEL E or beginner-Level I learners.
Students using this book can play these pieces hands separate or together!
A level chart is included in the back of this book.

DO'S AND DON'TS FOR PIANO:

WASH YOUR HANDS BEFORE YOU PLAY OR PRACTICE PIANO.

SIT TALL WITH YOUR FEET ON THE GROUND. IF THEY DON'T REACH, FIND SOME EMPTY BOXES TO REST YOUR FEET ON.

HOLD YOUR ARMS OUT SO THEY TOUCH THE FALLBOARD OF THE PIANO. IF YOUR ARMS ARE NOT PARALLEL WITH THE GROUND, FIND SOMETHING TO SIT ON TO MAKE YOURSELF TALLER LIKE A BOOSTER SEAT, CUSHION OR PILLOW.

LOOK AT WHERE YOUR FINGERS GO BEFORE YOU START THE PIECE

COUNT YOURSELF OFF BEFORE YOU START:
"1-2-READY-PLAY" OR "1-2-READY-GO"

KEEP YOUR FINGERS GLUED TO THE KEYS UNTIL YOU'RE DONE PLAYING

PLAYING ON A KEYBOARD IS FINE, HOWEVER STARTING ON A KEYBOARD THAT MAKES LOUD AND SOFT SOUNDS (HAS TOUCH RESPONSE) WILL HELP YOU MAKE MORE BEAUTIFUL MUSIC

IF YOU'RE FEELING WIGGLY SEE IF YOU CAN BALANCE A STUFFED ANIMAL ON YOUR HEAD FOR 10 SECONDS!

CURVE YOUR FINGERS WHEN YOU PLAY PIANO LIKE YOU'RE CATCHING A BUBBLE!

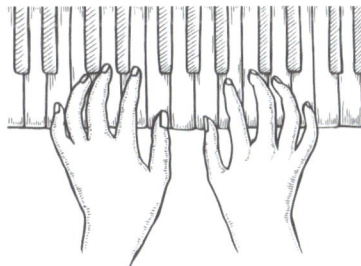

WHOLE NOTE

"WHOLE NOTE HOLD IT"
4 BEATS

HALF NOTE

"HOLD ME"
2 BEATS

QUARTER NOTE

"QUARTER"
1 BEAT

BASS CLEF

USE YOUR LEFT HAND
TO PLAY THESE NOTES

SHARP

RAISES A NOTE 1/2 STEP
TO THE RIGHT

FLAT

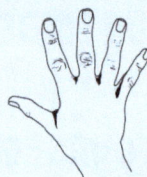

LOWERS A NOTE 1/2
TO THE LEFT

RIGHT HAND

USE THIS HAND TO
PLAY TREBLE CLEF

TREBLE CLEF

USE YOUR RIGHT HAND
TO PLAY THESE NOTES

LEFT HAND

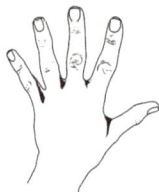

USE THIS HAND TO PLAY
BASS CLEF NOTES

HALF REST

HOLD 2 BEATS

QUARTER REST

HOLD 1 BEAT

REPEAT SIGN

PLAY AGAIN

DOUBLE BAR LINE

THE END OF THE
PIECE

NATURAL

NOTE RETURNS
TO THE
"NORMAL" PLACE

BAR LINE

CREATES MEASURES
DON'T STOP!

DOTTED HALF NOTE

"HOLD ME PLEASE"
THREE BEATS

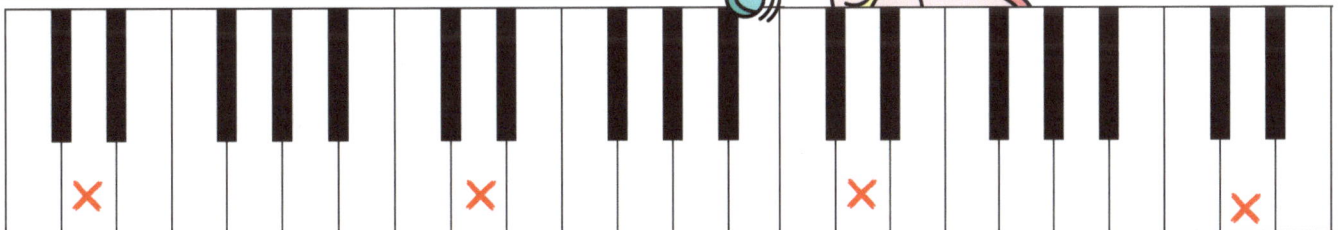

6

THAT'S GREAT, NOW HOW ABOUT YOUR HOMEWORK?

I PRACTICED JINGLE BELLS!

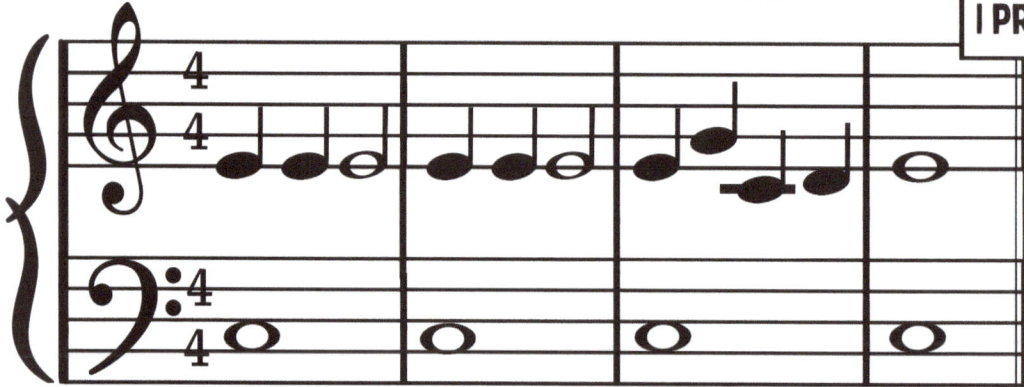

AXEL! THAT HASN'T BEEN HOMEWORK SINCE DECEMBER!

I KNOW, BUT I JUST LOVE THAT SONG!
BUT I ALSO TURNED JINGLE BELLS INTO HALLOWEEN MUSIC!
SEE ALL THE ORANGE ARROWS? THAT MEANS TO PLAY THE BLACK KEY
TO THE LEFT OF E. IT MAKES IT SOUND SPOOKY!

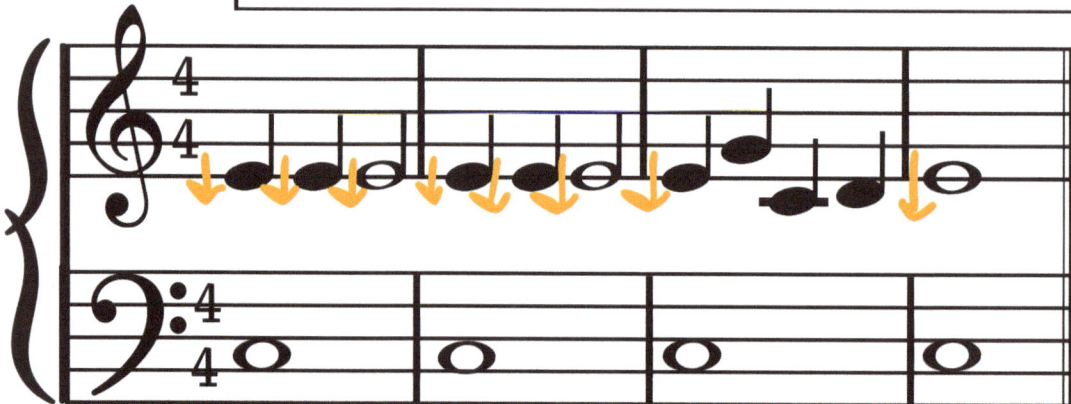

AXLE, THAT IS AMAZING! THIS IS EXACTLY
WHAT I WANTED TO TEACH YOU ABOUT TODAY!

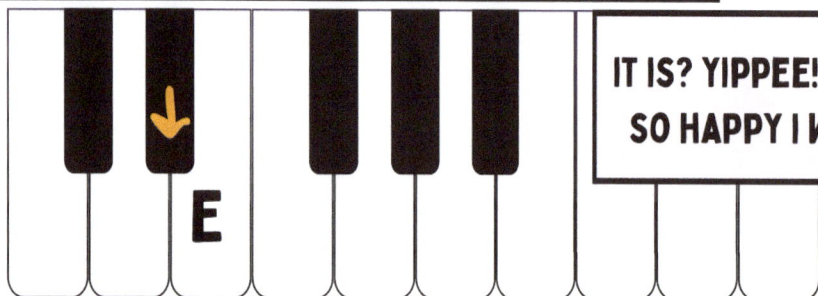

IT IS? YIPPEE! THAT MAKES ME
SO HAPPY I WANT TO BOUNCE!

E

HEY AXLE, THERE'S A **SECRET CODE** THAT MUSICIANS USE INSTEAD OF THOSE ORANGE ARROWS, AND IT WILL MAKE YOUR MUSIC EASIER TO READ! THIS SYMBOL IS CALLED **A FLAT** AND INSTEAD OF WRITING IT BEFORE **EVERY** NOTE, YOU CAN JUST WRITE IT **ONCE** AT THE BEGINNING OF EACH MEASURE TO LOWER A NOTE A 1/2 STEP. IT LOOKS LIKE A SMOOSHED LETTER B. TRY IT!

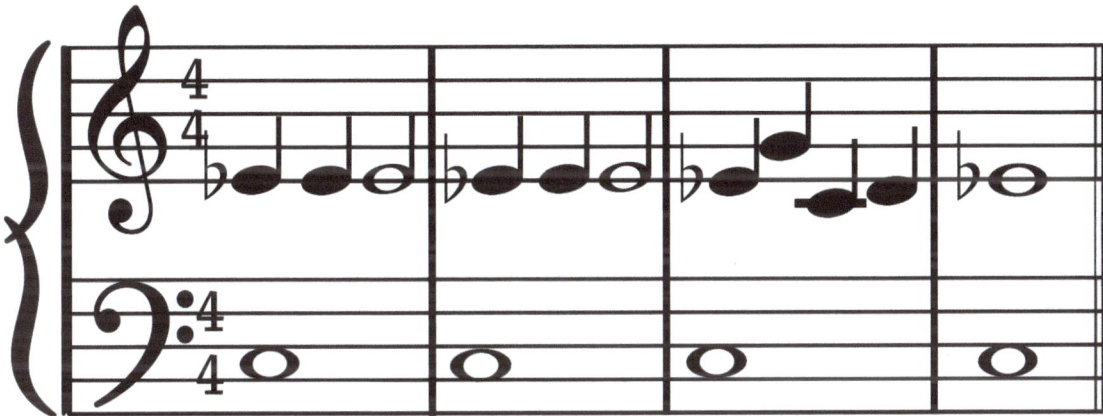

WOW! THAT IS ALOTOL EASIER! AND I DON'T HAVE TO WRITE THEM ON EVERY NOTE !

YOU CAN USE FLATS TO MAKE ALMOST ALL THE MUSIC YOU'VE LEARNED SOUND "SPOOKY". WE CALL SPOOKY, SAD OR MELANCHOLY SOUNDING MUSIC "MINOR." WHEN THE MUSIC SOUNDS HAPPY WE CALL THAT "MAJOR!" NOW ABOUT YOUR LESSON...

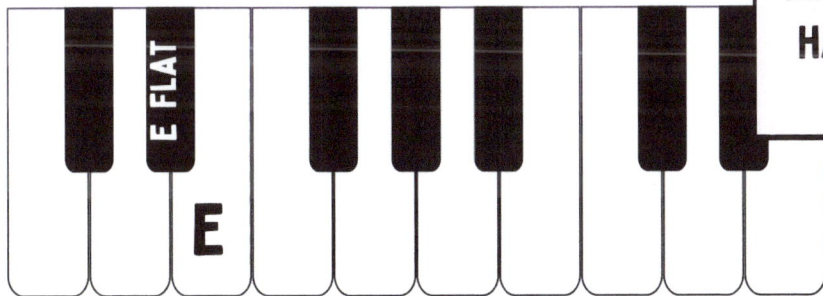

HEY, TEACHER, I HAVE ANOTHER QUESTION!

E FLAT

E

HOW CAN I MAKE A NOTE GO HIGHER? IS THERE A SECRET CODE FOR THAT?

STOP BOUNCING FOR A BIT AND I'LL SHOW YOU A SHARP SYMBOL

OH SURE, I KNOW THIS! I PLAY SHARP ALL THE TIME WITH MY BEST FRIEND OCTAVIUS!

YOU'RE THINKING OF TIC-TAC-TOE: THAT'S A GAME. SHARPS ARE ANOTHER SECRET CODE OF MUSICIANS!

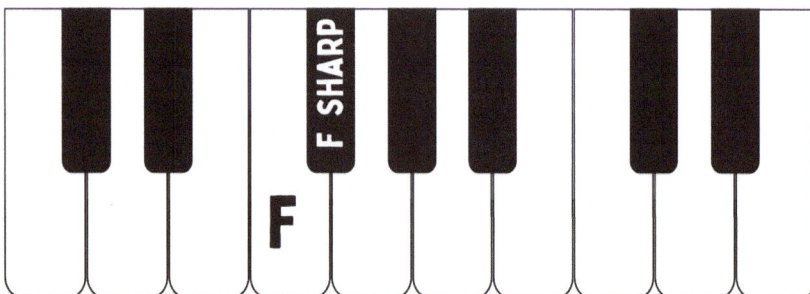

F SHARP

F

SHARP

A SHARP MAKES A NOTE HIGHER BY A 1/2 STEP. WHEN YOU SEE THIS SYMBOL YOU'LL PLAY THE KEY 1/2 STEP HIGHER-TO THE RIGHT.

AXLE-AWESOME! I CAN'T WAIT TO TRY IT OUT IN THIS PIRATE SONG I MADE UP YESTERDAY. CAN YOU HELP ME WRITE THOSE SHARP THINGYS IN?

SURE: SHARPS ARE PRETTY EASY TO WRITE: TWO STRAIGHT LEGS AND THE ARMS GO UP AND TO THE RIGHT LIKE A DAB!

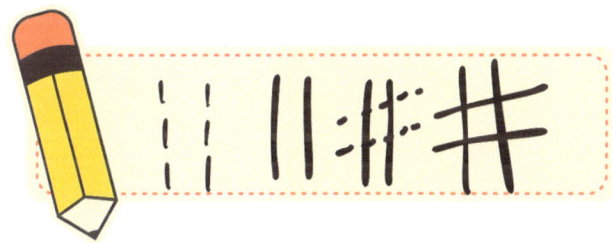

YO HO HO AND A BOTTLE OF CHUM, WITH

YOU MY FRIEND WE WILL LAUGH 'TILL WE'RE DONE!

AXEL'S WORKOUT MUSIC

8VA------------

HELP AXEL DRAW SHARPS IN FRONT OF THESE SPACE NOTES, THEN WRITE THE NAME OF THE NOTE IN THE BOX!

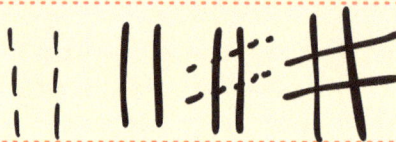

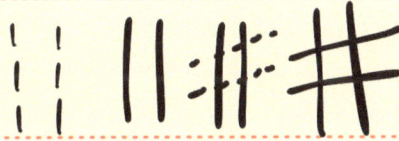

WOW, THAT'S A GREAT WAY TO USE SHARPS! NOW, ABOUT YOUR HOMEWORK FROM LAST WEEK....

SURE, BUT FIRST I HAVE ANOTHER QUESTION...

YES AXLE.....

WHAT IF I DON'T WANT THE NOTE TO BE SHARP OR FLAT ANYMORE? CAN I JUST WRITE "NO" IN FRONT OF THE NOTE?

THAT'S ACTUALLY A GREAT QUESTION! THERE IS ONE MORE SPECIAL SYMBOL I NEED TO TEACH YOU FIRST...

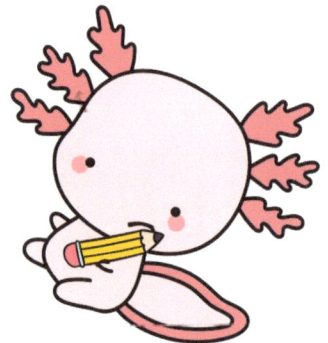

SPECIAL SYMBOL? LIKE AN EMOJI?

NOPE! THE LAST SECRET CODE MUSICIANS USE IS CALLED A NATURAL. IT TURNS A NOTE BACK TO NORMAL! LIKE WHEN YOU TAKE OFF YOUR HALLOWEEN COSTUME!

OH SURE, THAT MAKES SENSE. REMEMBER LAST YEAR WHEN I DRESSED UP LIKE A ZOMBIE? THIS YEAR I WANT TO BE A WITCH!

YES, I REMEMBER YOUR HALLOWEEN COSTUMES, BUT LET'S GET BACK TO MUSIC! TO DRAW A NATURAL SIGN YOU START BY DRAWING A LETTER L

I'M GOOD AT THOSE THERE ARE ALOTL IN MY NAME!

VERY FUNNY! THE NEXT STEP IS TO DRAW AN UPSIDE DOWN L. THIS PART IS TRICKY SO LOOK AT MY EXAMPLE CAREFULLY.

AND THAT'S ALL I HAVE TO DO TO MAKE THE NOTE NORMAL? THAT'S EASY!

SURE, JUST REMEMBER THAT A BAR LINE ERASES ALL THE FLATS AND SHARPS TOO, SO YOU ONLY NEED A NATURAL IF IT'S IN THE SAME MEASURE WITH A FLAT OR SHARP BEFORE IT.

NO WORRIES, CHECK THIS OUT:
SEE THE BIG PINK ERASERS ON THE
BAR LINES? IMAGINE THOSE ERASERS
ARE THERE ALL THE TIME, ERASING
YOUR SHARPS AND FLATS!

WHOA, I'M CONFUSSED.

HELP AXEL FIGURE OUT HOW MANY SHARPS OR FLATS ARE
IN EACH MEASURE, THEN WRITE THE NUMBER IN THE BOX

AXEL'S LULLABY

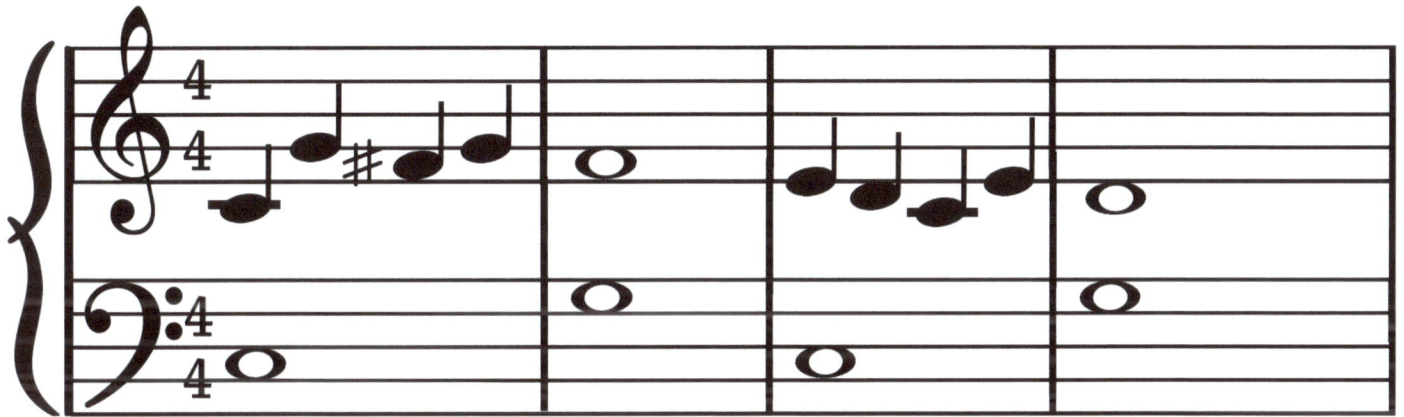

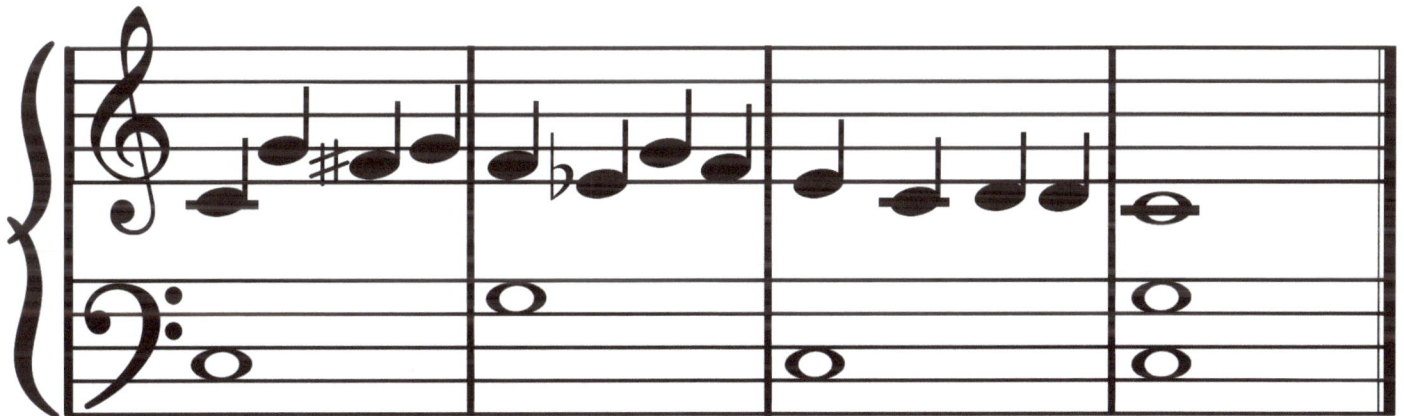

HEY AXEL, DON'T FALL ASLEEP! YOUR
LESSON IS ALMOST OVER THEN YOU
CAN GO HOME AND TAKE A NAP!

I'M AWAKE NOW!

HEY, I THINK I'VE GOT IT!

GREAT, NOW LET'S PLAY THIS PIECE THAT HAS ALOTL, I MEAN, A LOT OF ACCIDENTALS!

DID YOU SAY AXOLOTOLS?

NO, ACCIDENTALS! SAY "AX-I-DENT-TAILS." THAT'S WHAT WE CALL SHARPS, FLATS AND NATURALS.

SHARP-RAISES A NOTE 1/2 STEP

NATURAL-RETURN TO THE NORMAL KEY

FLAT-LOWERS A NOTE 1/2 STEP

SHARP LOOKOUT

Every time I play pi – a – no I will look for sharp signs!

I know that they make notes higher, and i draw just four lines.

Two lines go-ing down, up, two a-cross and up, yup!

Every time I play pi – a – no I will look for sharp signs!

Ev-ery time I practice i will know about these signs!

SHARP ATTACK

Thanks for | teach-ing | me ab-out these | sharps!

I | can't | wait to | teach my friend the | shark!

Just like a | sec-ret code, | I'm in | awe,

13

ea-sy as a | tic tac toe, | fun to | draw!

17

Thanks for | teach-ing | me ab-out these sharps!

21

Thank you | from the | bottom of my | heart!

NORMALIZE NATURALS

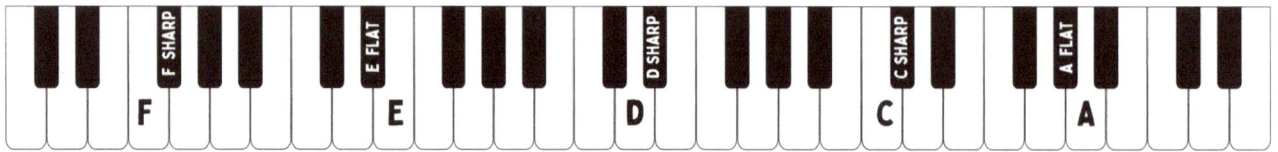

AXEL, I LOVED YOUR CONCERT, YOU
SOUNDED AMAZING! YOU'VE LEARNED
SO MUCH TODAY! JUST REMEMBER:
A SHARP MAKES A NOTE 1/2 STEP
HIGHER, A FLAT MAKES A NOTE 1/2 STEP
LOWER AND A NATURAL RETURNS THE
NOTE TO THE "NORMAL" PLACE.
NOW YOU JUST NEED TO PRACTICE YOUR
MUSIC THIS WEEK! OKAY!? AXEL?
AXEL.....

ACCIDENTAL MAZE

Help Axel find his way to his delicious fish dinner through the accidental maze by connecting the sharps, flats & naturals!

START HERE:

END HERE!

BOOK LEVEL CHART FOR THE **VERY FUN PIANO LIBRARY**

PIANO GRADE	FUN PIANO LEVEL	MAIN CONCEPTS
PRE-READING FINGER LEARNING-EVERY FINGER LABELLED	A	USE FINGERS 1-5, BLACK KEY PIECES LEARN PIANO KEYS 4 BASIC RHYTHMS
PRE-READING DIRECTIONAL READING (LESS FINGER NUMBERS)	B	RUNNING BUNNY EIGHTH NOTES REINFORCE KEY NAMES
PRE-READING NOTE LETTERS IN NOTE HEADS	C	BEGIN TO LEARN NOTE NAMES AND KEYBOARD LOCATION
NOTE READING	D	ONLY LANDMARK NOTES WITH LETTERS AND FINGERS LABELLED
NOTE READING	E	DECODE WHERE HANDS GO ON THE PIANO KEYBOARD

Violin Judy

Mrs. Judy Naillon, or "ViolinJudy" is a dedicated and enthusiastic independent piano and violin teacher, composer, and professional violinist. Her work consists of her large private music studio, as well as playing with her string quartet and Wichita Symphony Orchestra. She served as a church musician for over 20 years and is active in leadership in the musicians' union. She loves coming up with creative ideas to help both students and teachers be successful and blogs about it all at www.ViolinJudy.com and for Alfred's Music Publishers. When she is not writing new books she loves spending time with her family and little dog Pom.

CERTIFICATE
OF ACHIEVEMENT

This awarded to :

———————————————————

for the achievement of the completion of:

———————————————————

———————————   ———————————

Teacher   Date

www.ingramcontent.com/pod-product-compliance
Lightning Source LLC
LaVergne TN
LVHW072122070426

835511LV00002B/59